Biodiversity
of Rain Forests

GREG PYERS

Marshall Cavendish
Benchmark

New York

This edition first published in 2011 in the United States of America by
MARSHALL CAVENDISH BENCHMARK
An imprint of Marshall Cavendish Corporation

All rights reserved.

No part of this publication may be reproduced, stored in a retrieval system or transmitted, in any form or by any means, electronic, mechanical, photocopying, recording, or otherwise, without the prior permission of the copyright owner. Request for permission should be addressed to the Publisher, Marshall Cavendish Corporation, 99 White Plains Road, Tarrytown, NY 10591. Tel: (914) 332-8888, fax: (914) 332-1888.

Website: www.marshallcavendish.us

This publication represents the opinions and views of the author based on Greg Pyer's personal experience, knowledge, and research. The information in this book serves as a general guide only. The author and publisher have used their best efforts in preparing this book and disclaim liability rising directly and indirectly from the use and application of this book.

Other Marshall Cavendish Offices:
Marshall Cavendish Ltd. 5th Floor, 32-38 Saffron Hill, London EC1N 8 FH, UK • Marshall Cavendish International (Asia) Private Limited, 1 New Industrial Road, Singapore 536196 • Marshall Cavendish International (Thailand) Co Ltd. 253 Asoke, 12th Flr, Sukhumvit 21 Road, Klongtoey Nua, Wattana, Bangkok 10110, Thailand • Marshall Cavendish (Malaysia) Sdn Bhd, Times Subang, Lot 46, Subang Hi-Tech Industrial Park, Batu Tiga, 40000 Shah Alam, Selangor Darul Ehsan, Malaysia

Marshall Cavendish is a trademark of Times Publishing Limited

All websites were available and accurate when this book was sent to press.

Library of Congress Cataloging-in-Publication Data

Pyers, Greg.
    Biodiversity of rain forests / Greg Pyers.
        p. cm. — (Biodiversity)
    Includes index.
    Summary: "Discusses the variety of living things in a rain forest ecosystem"—Provided by publisher.
    ISBN 978-1-60870-073-8
    1. Rain forests—Juvenile literature. 2. Rain forest ecology—Juvenile literature.
    3. Endangered ecosystems—Juvenile literature. I. Title.
    QH86.P94 2010
577.34—dc22

                                                                        2009041732

First published in 2010 by
MACMILLAN EDUCATION AUSTRALIA PTY LTD
15–19 Claremont Street, South Yarra 3141

Visit our website at www.macmillan.com.au or go directly to www.macmillanlibrary.com.au

Associated companies and representatives throughout the world.

Copyright © Greg Pyers 2010

Edited by Georgina Garner
Text and cover design by Kerri Wilson
Page layout by Kerri Wilson
Photo research by Legend Images
Illustrations by Richard Morden

Printed in China

Acknowledgments
The author and the publisher are grateful to the following for permission to reproduce copyright material:

Front cover photograph of a scarlet macaw and a white-faced capuchin monkey sharing a tree limb, Osa Peninsula, Costa Rica, courtesy of Roy Toft/Getty Images.
Back cover photograph of a Ulysses butterfly © Vladimir Sazonov/Shutterstock.

Photographs courtesy of:
© Dr David Wachenfeld/AUSCAPE, 13; Andrew Holt/Getty Images, 21; Michael Nichols/Getty Images, 17; Beth Perkins/Getty Images, 25; Roy Toft/Getty Images, 1, 10; Photolibrary/Victor Englebert, 29; Photolibrary/Michael Fogden, 7, 22; Photolibrary/Max Milligan, 4; Picture Media/REUTERS/Nathalie van Vliet/Centre for International Forestry Research/Handout, 19; Picture Media/ REUTERS/Stringer, 18; © Ella_K/Shutterstock, 16; Tourism NSW, 23.

While every care has been taken to trace and acknowledge copyright, the publisher tenders their apologies for any accidental infringement where copyright has proved untraceable. Where the attempt has been unsuccessful, the publisher welcomes information that would redress the situation.

1 3 5 6 4 2

Contents

What Is Biodiversity?   4

Why Is Biodiversity Important?   6

Rain Forests of the World   8

Rain Forest Biodiversity   10

Rain Forest Ecosystems   12

Threats to Rain Forest Biodiversity   14

Biodiversity Threat: Farming   16

Biodiversity Threat: Wildlife Trade   18

Biodiversity Threat: Logging   20

Biodiversity Threat: Climate Change   22

Rain Forest Conservation   24

Case Study: The Amazon Rain Forest   26

What Is the Future of Rain Forests?   30

Glossary   31

Index   32

Glossary Words

When a word is printed in **bold**, you can look up its meaning in the Glossary on page 31.

What Is Biodiversity?

Biodiversity, or biological diversity, describes the variety of living things in a particular place, in a particular **ecosystem**, or across the entire Earth.

Measuring Biodiversity

The biodiversity of a particular area is measured on three levels:

- **species** diversity, which is the number and variety of species in the area.
- genetic diversity, which is the variety of **genes** each species has. Genes determine the characteristics of different living things. A variety of genes within a species enables it to **adapt** to changes in its environment.
- ecosystem diversity, which is the variety of **habitats** in the area. A diverse ecosystem has many habitats within it.

Species Diversity

Some ecosystems, such as coral reefs and rain forests, have very high species diversity. One scientific study found 534 species in just 54 square feet (5 square meters) of coral reef in the Caribbean Sea. In the Amazon Rain Forest, in South America, 50 species of ants and many other species were found in just 11 square feet (1 sq m) of leaf litter. In desert habitats, an area of the same size might be home to as few as ten species.

Macaws live in rain forest habitats and are part of rain forest biodiversity.

Habitats and Ecosystems

Rain forests are habitats, which are places where plants and animals live. Within a rain forest habitat, there are also many different types of smaller habitats, sometimes called microhabitats. Some rain forest microhabitats are the rain forest floor, the tree trunks, and the treetops. Different kinds of **organisms** live in these places. The animals, plants, other living things, nonliving things, and all the ways they affect each other make up a rain forest ecosystem.

Biodiversity Under Threat

The variety of species on Earth is under threat. There are somewhere between 5 million and 30 million species on Earth. Most of these species are very small and hard to find, so only about 1.75 million have been described and named. These are called known species.

Scientists estimate that as many as fifty species become **extinct** every day. Extinction is a natural process, but human activities have sped up the rate of extinction by nearly one thousand times.

Did You Know?

About 95 percent of all known animal species are invertebrates, which are animals without backbones, such as insect, worm, spider, and mollusc species. Vertebrates, which are animals with backbones, make up the remaining 5 percent.

Known Species of Organisms on Earth

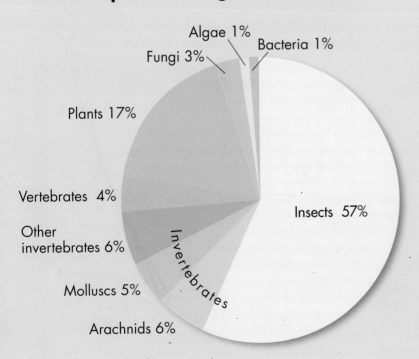

Algae 1%
Bacteria 1%
Fungi 3%
Plants 17%
Vertebrates 4%
Other invertebrates 6%
Insects 57%
Invertebrates
Molluscs 5%
Arachnids 6%

Approximate Numbers of Known Vertebrate Species	
ANIMAL GROUP	KNOWN SPECIES
Fish	31,000
Birds	10,000
Reptiles	8,800
Amphibians	6,500
Mammals	5,500

The known species of organisms on Earth can be divided into bacteria, algae, fungi, plant, and animal species. Animal species are further divided into vertebrates and invertebrates.

Why Is Biodiversity Important?

Biodiversity is important for many reasons. The diverse organisms in an ecosystem take part in natural processes essential to the survival of all living things. Biodiversity produces food and medicine. It is also important to people's quality of life.

Natural Processes

Human survival depends on the natural processes that go on in ecosystems. Through natural processes, air and water is cleaned, waste is decomposed, **nutrients** are recycled, and disease is kept under control. Natural processes depend on the organisms that live in the soil, on the plants that produce oxygen and absorb **carbon dioxide**, and on the organisms that break down dead plants and animals. When species of organisms become extinct, natural processes may stop working.

Food

We depend on biodiversity for our food. The world's major food plants are grains, vegetables, and fruits. These plants have all been bred from plants in the wild. Wild plants are important sources of genes for breeding new disease-resistant crops. If these wild plants were to become extinct, their genes would be lost.

Medicine

About 40 percent of all prescription drugs come from chemicals that have been extracted from plants. Scientists discover new, useful plant chemicals every year. The National Cancer Institute discovered that 70 percent of plants found to have anticancer properties were rain forest plants.

When plant species become extinct, the chemicals within them are lost forever. The lost chemicals might have been important in making new medicines.

Did You Know?

Botanists have identified more than 1,600 rain forest plants that could be grown commercially as fruits or vegetables.

Quality of Life

Biodiversity is important to our quality of life. Animals and plants inspire wonder. They are part of our **heritage**. To many people who visit the Daintree Rain Forest in Australia, the first sight of a Ulysses butterfly is an unforgettable experience. In our own neighborhoods, the birds and animals we see every day add color and interest to our existence.

Animal species such as the Ulysses butterfly inspire people's wonder and imagination. This improves their quality of life.

Extinct Species

The Tahiti parakeet is one of many species that has become extinct, reducing Earth's biodiversity. The parakeet lived on the Pacific island of Tahiti. The first time Europeans saw this bird was in 1769, when explorer James Cook visited the island on HMS *Endeavour*. In the following years, Europeans brought rats and cats to the island. This drove the Tahiti parakeet to extinction by 1844. Today, all that remains are five dead specimens, three of which were probably collected by Cook.

Rain Forests of the World

Rain forests are thick, dense forests found in areas with high rainfall. They are found on all continents except Antarctica.

Types of Rain Forest

Rain forests can be grouped into two main types, **tropical** rain forests and **temperate** rain forests. These two types of rain forest differ in **climate** and in the number and types of plant and animal species. **Conifers** dominate the cool temperate rain forests along the western coast of North America. Tropical rain forests, such as those in Central and South America, have mostly tall broad-leaved trees, ferns, and vines. Tropical rain forests have greater biodiversity than temperate rain forests.

Tropical and Temperate Rain Forests

RAIN FOREST TYPE	PLANT BIODIVERSITY	VERTEBRATE BIODIVERSITY	AGE	TOTAL AREA OF COVERAGE	CLIMATE
Tropical	Up to 80 tree species per acre, many vines, many **epiphytes**, and many trees with **buttress roots**	Many species at each layer	Millions of years	2.4 million square miles (6.3 million square kilometers), or 0.2% of the Earth's land area	High rainfall, warm to hot climate, and wet and dry seasons
Temperate	Up to 8 tree species per acre, few or no vines, many epiphytes, and no trees with buttress roots	Most species are ground-dwelling	Thousands of years	Less than 11,600 square miles (30,000 sq km), or 0.01% of Earth's land area	High rainfall, cold temperatures from autumn to spring, and cool summers

Where Rain Forests Are Found

Moisture is essential to the survival of rain forest plants. Tropical rain forests are found in the **humid** climates between the Tropic of Cancer and the Tropic of Capricorn. Temperate rain forests lie in the temperate zones, between the tropics and the colder areas of the poles. Temperate rain forests are found close to the coast, where fogs drift in from the sea and keep the warm summer air moist.

This map shows the location of Earth's tropical rain forests and temperate rain forests.

Cool Temperate and Warm Temperate Rain Forests

Cool temperate rain forests are found in places such as British Columbia, in Canada, and Alaska, where winter temperatures are very cold. Conifers such as Douglas firs and redwoods are the dominant tree species. These plants have tough leaves that can withstand freezing winter temperatures. In the warm temperate rain forests of Australia, broad-leaved trees are dominant.

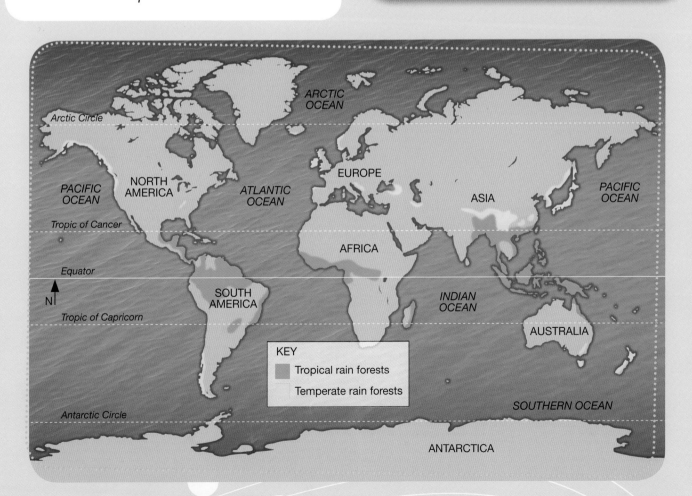

Arctic Circle

ARCTIC OCEAN

PACIFIC OCEAN

NORTH AMERICA

ATLANTIC OCEAN

EUROPE

ASIA

PACIFIC OCEAN

Tropic of Cancer

AFRICA

Equator

N

SOUTH AMERICA

INDIAN OCEAN

Tropic of Capricorn

AUSTRALIA

KEY
Tropical rain forests
Temperate rain forests

SOUTHERN OCEAN

Antarctic Circle

ANTARCTICA

Rain Forest Biodiversity

More species live in rain forests than in any other type of habitat. Tropical rain forests are particularly high in biodiversity. Life thrives in the different layers of the rain forest.

Full of Life

Rain forests cover about 6 percent of Earth's surface yet they are home to two-thirds of the world's species of plants and animals. In one study of a rain forest in Peru, researchers found 283 tree species growing in just 2.5 acres (1 hectare). In the United States and Canada, there are just 700 tree species total. In all of Europe, there are 320 butterfly species, but the rain forests of Manu National Park in Peru are home to 1,300 butterfly species.

Tropical Rain Forest Biodiversity

Within a tropical rain forest, there are many different microhabitats. Life thrives in the warm, humid climate of the tropics. Because there are so many species in a tropical rain forest, there are many **interactions** between them, making rain forest ecosystems very complex.

Tropical rain forests are millions of years old, so there has been a long time for many species to **evolve** to survive in their habitats. Rain forests in temperate regions are younger and they are not as biodiverse.

Many species live closely together and interact with each other in rain forest habitats.

Rain Forest Layers

A rain forest has several layers of **vegetation**. The lowest layer is the rain forest floor, where seedlings, mosses, lichens, and ferns grow. Above this layer is an understory of saplings and vines. The next layer is the rain forest **canopy**, which is formed by the leaves of the tall trees. Even taller trees, called emergent trees, reach above the canopy.

Each layer of vegetation in a rain forest supports different animal species. In the Amazon Rain Forest spider monkeys may spend their entire lives in the canopy, where they can find fruits and leaves to eat. Tapirs remain on the rain forest floor. Other species, such as boa constrictors, move from one layer to another.

Tamarin Diversity

Tamarins are small monkeys native to South America. There are seventeen species of tamarin and each species inhabits relatively small areas of rain forest, usually in the understory and canopy layers. The golden lion tamarin is found in pockets of rain forest in eastern Brazil, the emperor tamarin is found in western Brazil, the pied tamarin is found in northern Brazil, and the cotton-top tamarin is found in Colombia.

EMERGENT LAYER

CANOPY

UNDERSTORY

vines

saplings

ferns

lichens

mosses

seedlings

FOREST FLOOR

There are four layers of vegetation in a tropical rain forest: the forest floor, the understory, the canopy, and the emergent layer.

Rain Forest Ecosystems

Living and nonliving things, and the interactions between them,
make up rain forest ecosystems. Living things are plants and animals.
Nonliving things include the soil, the leaf litter, and the climate.

Food Chains and Food Webs

A very important way that species interact is by eating or consuming other species.
This transfers energy and nutrients from one organism to another. A food chain
illustrates the flow of energy, by showing what eats what. A food web shows how
many different food chains fit together.

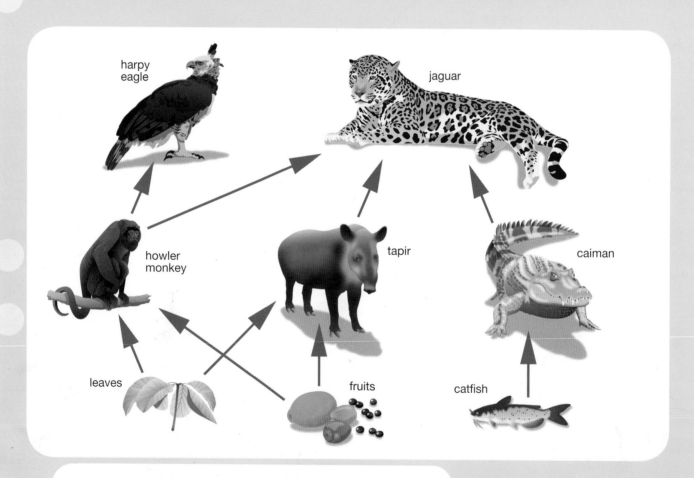

This Amazon Rain Forest food web is made up of several
food chains. In one food chain, fruits are eaten by tapirs,
which in turn are eaten by jaguars.

Other Interactions

Apart from eating and being eaten, living things in a rain forest interact in other ways, too. After high rainfall, rain forest rivers flood and fish swim over the rain forest floor to feed on fallen fruit. Seeds in the fruit are dispersed later in fish droppings.

Epiphytes

Epiphytes are plants that use the trunks and branches of other plants for support. This helps them grow high up where there is sunlight. In turn, epiphytes benefit other species. Some types of epiphytes, such as bromeliads, benefit animal species because the leaves form reservoirs where rain water collects. Monkeys, birds, and frogs use these pools of rain water.

Keystone Species

A keystone species is critical to the survival of many other species. In New Guinea and Australia, the southern cassowary feeds on the fruits of many rain forest plants. The seeds of these plants are spread in the bird's droppings. If the southern cassowary were to become extinct, many plants would not be able to spread and grow, affecting many animals that depend on these plants.

The southern cassowary is a keystone species because many other organisms depend on it for survival.

Threats to Rain Forests

Rain forests around the world are under threat from a range of human activities. Agriculture, logging, wildlife trade, and climate change put rain forests in danger. There is high biodiversity in rain forests and the survival of many species is in jeopardy.

Biodiversity Hotspots

There are about thirty-four regions in the world that have been identified as biodiversity hotspots. These are regions that have very high biodiversity that is under severe threat from humans.

Biodiversity hotspots have many species that are found nowhere else. These species are called **endemic species**. Because rain forests have both high biodiversity and a large number of endemic species, many rain forests are included within the biodiversity hotspots.

Examples of Biodiversity Hotspots that Include Rain Forest

HOTSPOT	RAIN FOREST BIODIVERSITY	MAJOR THREATS TO RAIN FOREST BIODIVERSITY
Sundaland (includes the islands of Borneo and Sumatra)	The hotspot contains 10% of the world's flowering plant species, 12% of the world's mammal species, 17% of the world's bird species, and more than 25% of the world's fish species. About 60% of its plant species are endemic.	Wildlife trade, logging, oil palm plantations
Chilean temperate rain forests	Many species are endemic to the hotspot, such as 35% of tree and shrub species, 23% of reptile species, 30% of bird species, 33% of mammal species, 50% of fish species, and 76% of amphibians.	Wildlife trade, pine and eucalypt plantations, fire, **invasive species**
Madagascar and Indian Ocean islands	Between 70% and 90% of species are endemic to the hotspot.	Wildlife trade, logging, land clearing for agriculture
Philippines	Thousands of species are endemic to the hotspot, and many of these are endangered, such as the Philippines eagle and the golden-capped fruit bat.	Wildlife trade, land clearing for agriculture

Deforestation

Deforestation occurs when forests are cleared for farming land or to build roads or towns. Rain forests are also logged for their lumber, and so that animals can be hunted.

Rates of Deforestation

About 5,000 years ago, there may have been 9 million square miles (24 million sq km) of tropical rain forests on Earth. By 1950 there was less than half of this left. There is 2.4 million square miles (6.25 million sq km) of rain forest remaining today. It is being cut down at a rate of around 60,000 square miles (160,000 sq km) a year. The temperate rain forests of Europe have long been cleared and 95 percent of North America's temperate rain forests have been cleared.

Where Deforestation Occurs

The largest areas of rain forest being cleared are mainly in those countries that still have relatively large areas of rain forest remaining. These countries are often poor countries that rely on export income from their rain forests or that have large populations that rely on **slash-and-burn farming** to grow crops.

Causes of Tropical Rain Forest Deforestation, 2000–2005

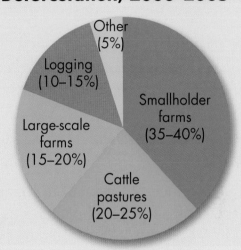

Other (5%)
Logging (10–15%)
Large-scale farms (15–20%)
Cattle pastures (20–25%)
Smallholder farms (35–40%)

Logging and farming cause 95 percent of deforestation. Other causes include forest fires and the building of towns and cities.

Rates of Rain Forest Clearing in 20 Tropical Countries, 2000–2005

Average Area Cleared Each Year (millions of acres)

8.75
7.5
6.25
5.0
3.75
2.5
1.25
0

Brazil, Indonesia, Burma (Myanmar), Zambia, Tanzania, Nigeria, Dem. Rep. of the Congo, Zimbabwe, Venezuela, Bolivia, Mexico, Cameroon, Cambodia, Ecuador, Paraguay, Philippines, Honduras, Ethiopia, Malaysia, Papua New Guinea

Countries

BIODIVERSITY THREAT:
Farming

In many parts of the world, large areas of rain forest have been cleared to grow crops, such as oil palm, and to graze livestock. Today, rain forest continues to be cleared for farming and agriculture. Some rain forest is cleared for slash-and-burn farming.

Palm Oil Plantations

Rain forests are cleared to make way for palm oil plantations. Palm oil is the most-consumed vegetable oil in the world. It is extracted from the fruit of the oil palm, a tree native to western Africa. It is used to make margarine, soap, cosmetics, cookies, and many other products. Palm oil is also used as a biofuel, meaning it can be used to run vehicle engines.

Indonesia produces 45 percent of the world's palm oil. About 27,000 square miles (70,000 sq km) of palm oil plantations have been planted. This is expected to triple by 2020. On the islands of Sumatra and Borneo, the clearing of rain forest for palm oil production is a major threat to many rain forest species, most notably the orangutan.

Sustainable Palm Oil

Major companies that use palm oil in their products have begun to use only palm oil that has been produced sustainably, from plantations grown on existing farmland. Sustainable products can be made without using up natural resources. Buying products that are made sustainably helps stop rain forest clearing.

Large areas of rain forest are cleared to make room for palm oil plantations.

Slash-and-Burn Farming

The slash-and-burn method of farming has been used for thousands of years. It involves clearing an area of forest, then burning the vegetation. Nutrients in the leaves and branches fertilize the soil and the crops that are eventually planted. After a few years, however, the soil is too poor for crops and so more rain forest is cleared.

In the past, about 2.5 acres (1 ha) of rain forest would be cleared by villagers growing food crops and the forest would be given time to recover. Today, with much higher populations, slash-and-burn farming accounts for half of the annual clearing of tropical rain forests. The crops grown are not always for food production. Since the 1990s about 150 square miles (400 sq km) of rain forest in Colombia has been slashed and burned each year to grow opium poppy, coca, and cannabis to make illegal drugs.

Burning Rain Forests in the Past

Some countries have a long history of burning rain forests. For example, humans arrived in Australia at least 50,000 years ago, when rain forests still covered much of northeastern Australia. These indigenous Australians used fire to open up the country and attract grazing animals, such as kangaroos, for hunting. Burning also encouraged the growth of important food plants. Over time, this burning shrunk the area of rain forests and encouraged the spread of fire-tolerant eucalypt forests.

The Amazon Rain Forest is cleared by fire for farming crops and grazing animals.

BIODIVERSITY THREAT:
Wildlife Trade

The illegal trade in wildlife is worth billions of dollars. After drugs, diamonds, and weapons, reptiles are the fourth most valuable commodity smuggled. Wildlife trade seriously threatens many rain forest species.

Collectors

Most animals that are **poached** from rain forests are sold to collectors overseas. The rarer a species is, the more a collector will pay for it. The endangered Sumatran elephant, a rain forest animal, is poached for the ivory in its tusks.

Did You Know?

The endangered Sumatran tiger is hunted so that its body parts can be sold and used in traditional Chinese medicines. Nearly every part of the tiger is used. There is no scientific evidence that these medicines have any true scientific value.

A monkey in a cage in Burma (Myanmar) waits to be sold as a pet.

Pet Trade

Many animals are poached from rain forests and sold overseas as pets. Monkeys, apes, parrots, and reptiles such as lizards are most popular. In Borneo, about one thousand orangutans are poached each year to be sold. Many of these are young animals that are orphaned when their mothers are shot by poachers or plantation workers.

Bush Meat

Wild animals killed by people for food are called bush meat. The people who kill animals to sell as bush meat are usually workers from mining and logging companies. These people are poorly paid and they do this to make money and to feed themselves. They do not distinguish between endangered and non-endangered species. This practice is a huge problem in the rain forests of central Africa. In Ghana, an estimated 425,000 tons (385,000 tonnes) of bush meat are harvested each year to be sold in markets and to restaurants.

Killing animals for bush meat can cause them to die out, or become extinct. In Vietnam, the endangered golden-headed langur has been hunted because its meat is a delicacy and is said to have medicinal properties. It is thought that there are only about sixty-four of these monkeys left in the wild.

Bush Meat Prices

Up to six hundred endangered lowland gorillas are killed each year for bush meat. In 2006 in central Africa, a hunter earned $40 for a dead gorilla, $20 for a chimpanzee, and $5 for a monkey. This is a significant wage for a poor mining or logging employee.

A trader sells bush meat in Gabon, in western Africa.

BIODIVERSITY THREAT:
Logging

Rain forests have been harvested for their lumber for centuries. Today, logging continues to be a major threat to rain forests and their biodiversity.

The Logging Industry

Large-scale logging of unprotected rain forests is undertaken legally by logging companies. Usually, only the mature trees are cut down. As the trees fall, however, they smash the surrounding vegetation. The rain forest canopy is breached and sunlight reaches the ground. This dries out the rain forest floor, making fires more likely. When the logs are dragged out of the forest, even more damage is done to rain forest plants and the soil.

Roads are built for trucks to collect the lumber from the rain forest. These roads enable hunters to enter deep into the rain forest in search of animals to **poach**. The roads also allow invasive species, such as weeds, into the rain forest.

Ruthless Companies

Many international lumber companies pay poor countries for the right to log large areas of rain forests. These companies make huge profits. When the companies have taken the lumber, the local people are left without their rain forest.

Fifteen Highest Producers of Lumber Harvested Legally from Tropical Rain Forests, 2005

COUNTRY	TIMBER HARVESTED (CUBIC FEET)
Brazil	5,936,077,000
Malaysia	727,482,000
Nigeria	491,438,000
Indonesia	394,747,000
Mexico	270,757,000
Uganda	155,667,000
Democratic Republic of the Congo	148,286,000
Burma (Myanmar)	137,020,000
Gabon	127,132,000
Togo	117,244,000
Colombia	114,631,000
Cameroon	113,395,000
Tanzania	100,046,000
Sudan	95,914,000
Vietnam	88,286,000

Illegal Logging

Illegal logging is logging that occurs in areas that have been set aside as rain forest reserves. Illegal loggers work in remote areas that are very difficult to patrol. The amount of lumber harvested illegally is often many times more than the amount harvested legally by the logging industry. The amount of lumber legally harvested from the rain forests of the Democratic Republic of the Congo is probably only 20 percent of the total amount logged. The rest is taken illegally.

Illegal logging deprives poor countries of up to $15 billion a year. This money could be spent on rain forest conservation. It could also be used to educate people so that they can find jobs and no longer be dependent on money from logging companies.

Threat to Mountain Gorillas

The rain forests of Virunga National Park, in the Democratic Republic of Congo, in Africa, are one of the last habitats of the mountain gorilla. The forests are threatened by local people collecting wood to make charcoal, known as *makala*. Charcoal is used for cooking and heating. Forest rangers are often threatened with violence when they confront people collecting wood inside the park.

Workers load logged rain forest trees onto a truck in Sumatra, in Indonesia. Legal and illegal logging is destroying the rain forest habitat of the Sumatran orangutan.

BIODIVERSITY THREAT:
Climate Change

The world's average temperature is rising because of increasing levels of certain gases, called greenhouse gases, in Earth's atmosphere. These gases trap heat, and the increasing temperature causes changes in the climate. These changes will affect rain forests.

Effects of Climate Change

Scientists are uncertain exactly how rain forests will be affected by climate change. They do know that the amount of rainfall and where it falls will change. If rainfall in a rain forest declines, the rain forest may gradually become a woodland, with fewer plant and animal species.

Global warming is causing polar ice caps to melt and the world's sea level to rise. As this happens, low-lying rain forests, such as in the Sundarbans of Bangladesh, will be flooded.

Did You Know?

One species of toucan, the keel-billed toucan, prefers lowland rain forest. It is now moving into mountain rain forests as temperatures are becoming warmer. The population of these toucans is increasing.

Effects on Animal Species

Climate change will affect rain forest animals in different ways. In Costa Rica, in Central America, the golden toad lived in a small area of mountain rain forest that was usually covered in clouds. The cloud kept the toad's habitat damp and fit to live in. As average temperatures rose, the cloud-cover began to lift on many summer days. The toad was unable to survive and it has not been seen since 1989.

The golden toad became extinct because of climate changes in its rain forest habitat.

Climate Change in the Past

Scientists look to the past to help make predictions about the effects of climate change. Forty million years ago, much of Australia, Antarctica, and South America was covered in rain forest. They were joined together as part of a supercontinent called Gondwana. As Gondwana broke up, Australia drifted north. Slowly and gradually, over thousands of years, its climate became drier and its rain forests began to shrink in area. Grasslands, woodlands, and eucalyptus forest grew in their place.

Scientists think the rate of climate change is much faster today. Many species will have too little time to adapt to climate changes and will become extinct.

The plants and animals of the Gondwana Rain Forests of eastern Australia evolved from those of the ancient Gondwana supercontinent. The plant and animal species in the rain forest today are suited to the changed climate.

Rain Forest Conservation

Conservation is the protection, preservation, and wise use of resources. Rain forests are a valuable resource. Research, education, laws, and replanting projects are very important in rain forest conservation plans.

The Importance of Rain Forests

Rain forests are a very important for many reasons. Rain forests:

- are habitat for more animal species than any other habitat

- are a rich source of plants and chemicals that can be used to make medicines

- have existed for thousands and even millions of years

- are impressive places to visit.

How Rain Forests Affect Climate

Rain forests are very important for Earth's climate. They are an important part of the water cycle and the clearing of a rain forest affects rainfall patterns over a wide area.

Rain forests also absorb vast amounts of carbon dioxide, a greenhouse gas that adds to the greenhouse effect and to climate change. One acre (0.4 ha) of rain forest absorbs more than 800 pounds (363 kilograms) of carbon from carbon dioxide each year. Rain forests convert the carbon dioxide to carbon, a major component of wood. When rain forests are burned, the carbon is released back into the atmosphere as carbon dioxide.

Conserving Temperate Rain Forest

The Great Bear Rain Forest, in British Columbia, Canada, is the world's largest temperate rain forest. On April 29, 2008, laws were passed to ban logging and to protect fifty-five large areas of this forest. These areas, called conservancies, were selected especially to conserve the rain forest's biodiversity.

Research

Research surveys or studies are used to find out about rain forests, such as how rain forest ecosystems work and how humans affect them. Research helps people find ways to conserve rain forests. The people who carry out this research are scientists who are employed by governments, universities, botanical gardens, zoos, or conservation organizations such as the World Wide Fund for Nature (WWF).

Education

Educating people about rain forests is essential for rain forest conservation. Information from scientists must be passed on to other people, including schoolchildren, farmers, and tourists. When people are shown how important rain forests are to their own lives, they are more likely to help conserve them.

Did You Know?

In 2008, Wildlife Conservation Society researchers discovered an estimated 125,000 western lowland gorillas deep in the remote northern rain forests of the Republic of the Congo. Until 2008, the world's population of this critically endangered species was thought to be around 50,000.

A scientist tests leaves in a rain forest in Costa Rica, in Central America. Scientific research can help discover ways to conserve rain forests.

CASE STUDY:
The Amazon Rain Forest

The Amazon Rain Forest is the largest rain forest in the world. The rain forest covers a total area of 3.1 million square miles (8.2 million sq km), which is about the size of the United States. The Amazon Rain Forest's biodiversity is remarkably high.

Threats to the Amazon Rain Forest's Biodiversity

Deforestation is the greatest threat to the Amazon Rain Forest's biodiversity. Without their rain forest habitat, animals have nowhere to live. The illegal wildlife trade is also a major threat.

Fires

Satellite photographs show that as many as 70,000 fires burned in the Amazon Rain Forest in 2007. Farmers and ranchers lit the fires, which were near roads. The construction of roads brings settlers and quickens the rate of deforestation.

Numbers of Known Species in the Amazon Rain Forest

SPECIES	NUMBER OF KNOWN SPECIES IN THE AMAZON RAIN FOREST	COMPARISON
Freshwater fish	At least 3,000	More fish species than in the entire Atlantic Ocean
Insects	At least 560,000	There are about 900,000 known insect species on Earth
Butterflies	At least 7,500	There are about 65 species of butterflies in Britain
Mammals	At least 427	Europe has 260 mammal species
Birds	At least 1,294	Australia has 800 bird species
Reptiles	At least 378	There are about 8,800 known reptile species in the world
Amphibians	At least 427	There are about 6,500 known amphibian species in the world
Plants	At least 40,000	There are about 298,000 known plant species in the world

Deforestation in the Amazon

Between 2000 and 2008, more than 58,000 square miles (150,000 sq km) of rain forest were cleared in Brazil. Rain forest is cleared for cattle ranching and for timber. The rate of deforestation, however, has been falling in recent years.

About 60 percent of deforestation in the Amazon Rain Forest is for grazing and cattle ranching. **Savanna** grasses are sown on the cleared land and herds of cattle are brought in to graze. Profits are made on the beef from these animals, most of which is exported overseas.

According to the conservation organization Greenpeace, between 60 percent and 80 percent of all lumber taken from the Amazon Rain Forest in Brazil is logged illegally. Loggers select valuable trees, such as mahogany and samauma. By removing certain species of trees, loggers change the rain forest ecosystem.

More than half of the Amazon Rain Forest is in Brazil.

Deforestation in the Brazilian Amazon Rain Forest, 1988–2008

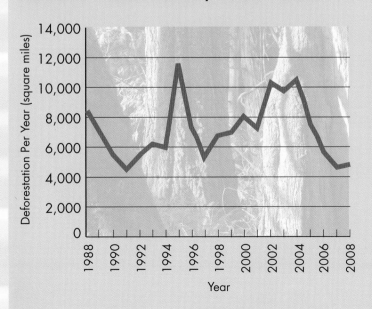

Wildlife Trade

Each year, anywhere between 9 million and 23 million birds, mammals, frogs, and reptiles are collected from the Amazon Rain Forest and smuggled overseas. Around 90 percent of these animals die before they reach their destinations. Rare and colorful birds, such as the blue-throated macaw and hyacinth macaw, are highly sought by collectors. The eggs of these and other bird species are also smuggled.

Some species are smuggled alive, but many other species are killed first. Caimans are killed for their skins, which are smuggled overseas to make handbags and shoes.

Conservation of Amazon Biodiversity

Although large areas of rain forest are still being cleared and animals are still poached, there are large conservation areas that are protecting the Amazon Rain Forest and its biodiversity.

Amazon Region Protected Areas Program

In 2003, the Brazilian Government, WWF, and other organizations created the Amazon Region Protected Areas (ARPA) program. It is the world's largest tropical forest conservation program. The program aims to:

- establish 109,000 square miles (283,000 sq km) of new protected areas of rain forest
- improve the management of 48,000 square miles (125,000 sq km) of existing reserves
- establish 34,000 square miles (89,000 sq km) of rain forest reserves for local communities to live and work in.

As part of ARPA, the Brazilian government committed to ending deforestation in the Brazilian Amazon Rain Forest by 2020.

Conservation Laws

Rain forest reserves are protected by law, but the Amazon is a vast area and these laws have to be enforced. In Brazil, it is the task of IBAMA, the government environmental enforcement agency, to enforce conservation laws. Recently, the Brazilian government increased the number of IBAMA agents. It is the agents' job to catch illegal loggers and smugglers, who are then punished with heavy fines or prison sentences.

World's Largest Rain Forest Reserve

In 2007 a new 8,000-square-mile (20,000 sq km) national park was created in French Guiana. The park lies next to national parks in Brazil, creating a 46,000-square-mile (120,000 sq km) area of protected rain forest, which is the largest rain forest reserve in the world.

Sustainable Use of the Rain Forest

Sustainable use of the rain forest is using the rain forest in a way that does not destroy it. A study in Peru found that logging the rain forest earns about $400 per acre ($1,000 per ha), but for only one year. Collecting fruit and rubber from the same patch of rain forest earns $170 per acre ($420 per ha), year after year.

Governments and conservation organizations are working in the Amazon to help local people make money from the rain forest in sustainable ways.

Did You Know?

The biodiversity of the Central Amazon Conservation Complex is among the world's richest. The giant arapaima fish, the Amazonian manatee, the black caiman, many species of electric fish, and two species of river dolphin are found there.

Yanomami women collect food from the rain forest. The Yanomami people have lived sustainably in the Amazon Rain Forest for the past thousand years.

29

What Is the Future of Rain Forests?

Rain forests are under severe threat from human activities and rain forest biodiversity is falling. When threats are removed, this decline can be slowed or even halted. Some species may return to areas and so increase biodiversity.

What Can You Do For Rain Forests?

You can help protect rain forests in several ways:

- Find out about rain forests. Why are they important and what threatens them?
- If you live near a rain forest, join volunteer groups who replant cleared land with rain forest species.
- Become a responsible consumer. Do not litter or buy products that have been harvested from rain forests.
- If you are concerned about rain forests in your area, or in other areas, send a letter to or e-mail your local newspaper, your state congressperson, or local representative, and express your concerns. Know what you want to say, set out your argument, be sure of your facts, and ask for a reply.

Useful Websites

- **www.panda.org/what_we_do/where_we_work/amazon/**
  This website gives information about WWF's work in the Amazon Rain Forest, including the Amazon Region Protected Areas program.

- **www.biodiversityhotspots.org**
  This website has information about the richest and most threatened areas of biodiversity on Earth.

- **www.iucnredlist.org**
  The International Union for Conservation of Nature (IUCN) Red List has information about threatened plant and animal species.

Glossary

adapt   Change in order to survive.

buttress roots   Tree roots with upper parts that are exposed above the ground.

canopy   Leaves of the upper layer of plants in a forest or woodland.

carbon dioxide   A colorless and odorless gas produced by plants, animals, and the burning of coal and oil.

climate   The weather conditions in a certain region over a long period of time.

conifers   Group made up of trees that have evergreen leaves and bear cones.

deforestation   The clearing of forests or trees.

ecosystem   The living and nonliving things in a certain area and the interactions between them.

endemic species   Species found only in a particular area.

epiphytes   Plants that grow on other plants.

evolve   Change over time.

extinct   Having no living members.

genes   Segments of deoxyribonucleic acid (DNA) in the cells of a living thing, which determine characteristics.

habitats   Places where animals, plants, or other living things live.

heritage   Things we inherit and pass on to future generations.

humid   With a high level of water vapor in the atmosphere.

interactions   Actions that are taken together or that affect each other.

invasive species   Nonnative species that negatively affect their new habitats.

nutrients   Substances that are used by living things for growth.

organisms   Animals, plants, and other living things.

poached   Hunted or taken illegally.

savanna   Very open woodland with grass between the trees.

slash-and-burn farming   Method of clearing forest for farming by cutting down and burning off vegetation.

species   A group of animals, plants, or other living things that share the same characteristics and can breed with one another.

temperate   In a region or climate that has mild temperatures.

tropical   In the hot and humid region between the Tropic of Cancer and the Tropic of Capricorn.

vegetation   Plants.

Index

A

agriculture,   14, 16–17
Amazon Rain Forest,   4,
    11, 26–29, 30

B

biodiversity hotspots,   14,
    30
bush meat,   19

C

cattle ranching,   27
climate change,   14,
    22–23, 24
conservation,   21, 24–25,
    28–29

D

deforestation,   15, 27, 28

E

ecosystem diversity,   4, 6,
    12–13
ecosystems,   4, 6, 10,
    12–13, 25, 27
education,   21, 24, 25
endangered species,   14,
    18, 19, 25
endemic species,   14
epiphytes,   8, 13
extinct species,   5, 6, 7,
    13, 19, 22, 23

F

fires,   14, 17, 20, 27
food chains,   12
food webs,   12

G

genetic diversity,   4, 6
golden toad,   22
Gondwana,   23
gorillas,   19, 21, 25

H

habitats,   4, 10, 21, 22,
    24, 27

I

illegal logging,   21, 27, 28

K

keystone species,   13

L

laws,   24, 28
location of rain forests,   9
logging,   14, 15, 19,
    20–21, 24, 27, 28, 29

M

medicines,   6, 18, 19, 24
microhabitats,   4, 10

O

orangutans,   16, 18

P

palm oil,   14, 16
poaching,   18, 20, 28

R

rain forest layers,   10, 11
research,   24, 25

S

slash-and-burn farming,
    15, 16, 17
species diversity,   4, 5,
    10, 11, 14, 22, 26, 29
Sumatran tiger,   18
sustainability,   16, 29

T

Tahiti parakeet,   7
tamarins,   11
temperate rain forests,   8,
    9, 10, 14, 15, 24
threats to biodiversity,   5,
    14–15, 16–17, 18–19,
    20–21, 22–23, 27, 30
toucans,   22
tropical rain forests,   8,
    9, 10, 15, 17, 20

W

websites,   30
wildlife trade,   14, 18–19,
    27